READ TOGETH

All About Camels

EDventure
LEARNING

How to Use This Book

This book is part of our Read Together series, a collection of books designed to be enjoyed by a young reader paired with a more experienced reader, such as a parent, grandparent, or older sibling. Take turns reading out loud together.

The pages on the left side are meant for the younger reader. These pages use short, simple sentences and larger print. They are marked at the bottom of the page with the symbol shown at left.

The right-side pages are for the older reader. They contain paragraphs with longer sentences and more complex vocabulary. These pages are marked at the bottom of the page with the symbol shown at right.

Shared reading helps new readers gain confidence. It's also a great way for all ages to bond over books. We hope you enjoy this book as you Read Together.

Printed in the United States of America
Paperback ISBN: 978-1-64824-012-6

EDventure Learning LLC
5601 State Route 31 #1296
Clay, NY 13039

www.edventurelearning.com
Email us at hello@edventurelearning.com

Keep in touch!

FOLLOW US ON SOCIAL MEDIA

@edventurelearning

www.edventurelearning.com

Want freebies? Email us at **hello@edventurelearning.com** with the subject "Read Together" to join our newsletter and we'll send you free printables to keep the learning going!

All About Lions

All About Penguins

All About Polar Bears

All About Tigers

All About Zebras

Printed in Great Britain
by Amazon

55635222R00018

Table of Contents

What Camels Look Like

Camels are large animals with brown fur.

Camels stand on four long, thin legs. Full-grown camels are 5-7 feet (1.5-2.1 meters) tall at shoulder height. They have long, curved necks.

Camels have humps on their backs.

Dromedary camels

There are two types of camels- dromedary and Bactrian. **Dromedary camels** have one hump, while **Bactrian camels** have two humps.

Camels' humps are made of fat. When there is not enough food or water, camels use this stored fat to give their bodies the energy they need to survive. The size of a camel's hump can change depending on how much food the camel eats. When a camel hasn't eaten and has to use up the fat stored in its hump, the hump can become smaller and floppy.

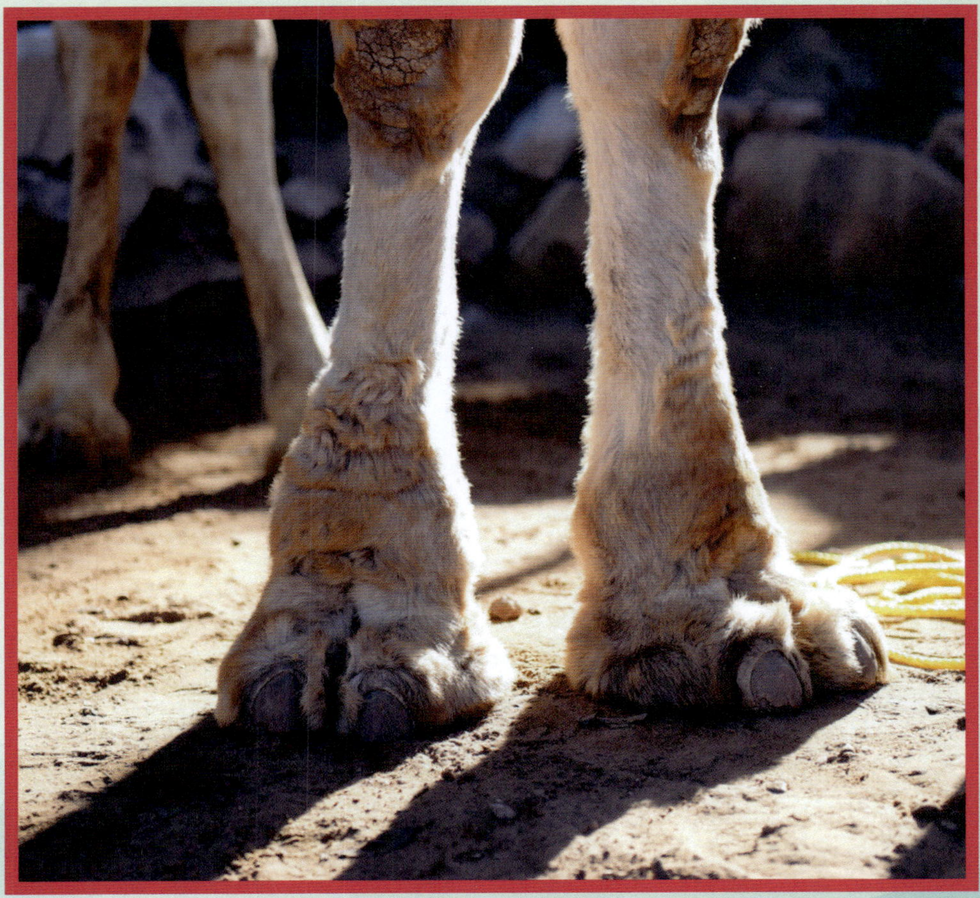

A camel's foot has two toes.

Camels have wide, flexible feet with two webbed toes. These help camels to balance on uneven ground and keep them from sinking into the sand. The soles of their feet have thick padding to protect them from heat.

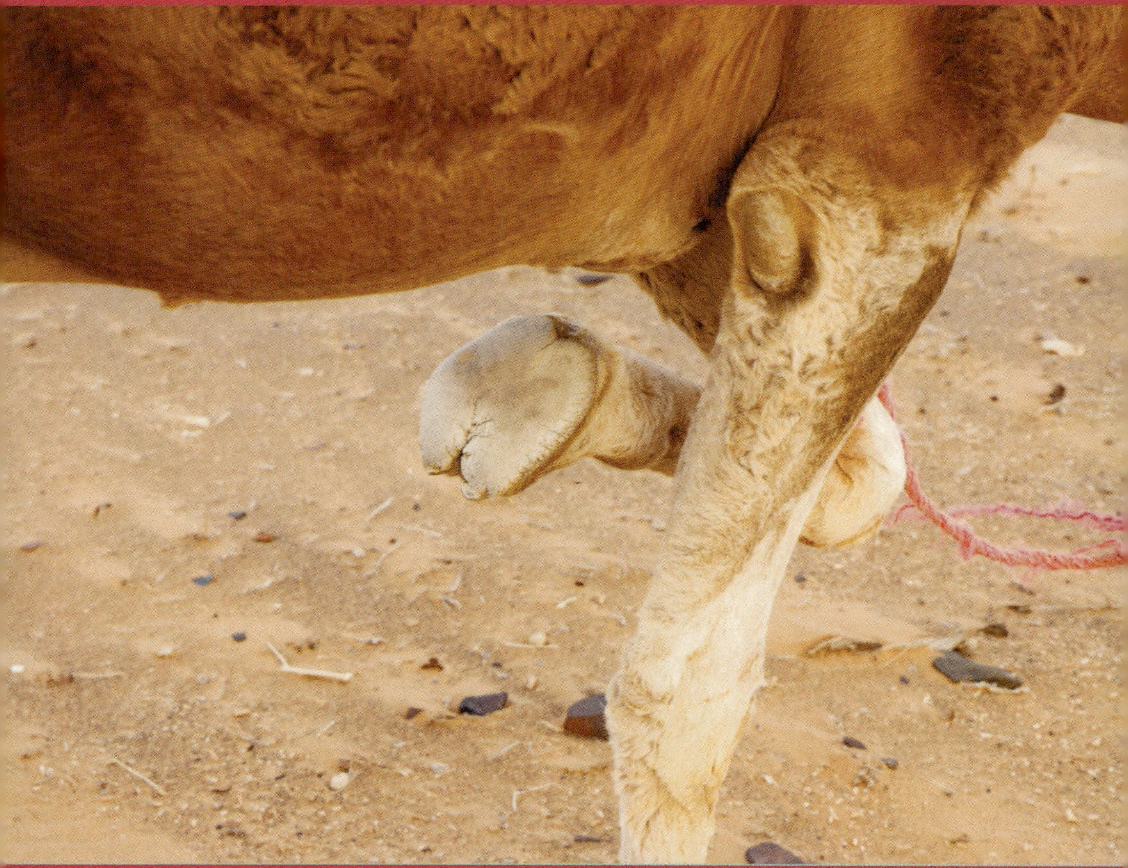

Their faces are made to keep out the sand.

Camels have two rows of long eyelashes that keep sand from getting into their eyes. Hair also protects the insides of their ears. In addition, camels can close their nostrils to keep out blowing sand.

Where Camels Live

Some camels live in hot, sandy deserts.

Dromedary camels live in the deserts of the Middle East. The land is sandy, and the climate is very hot and dry all year.

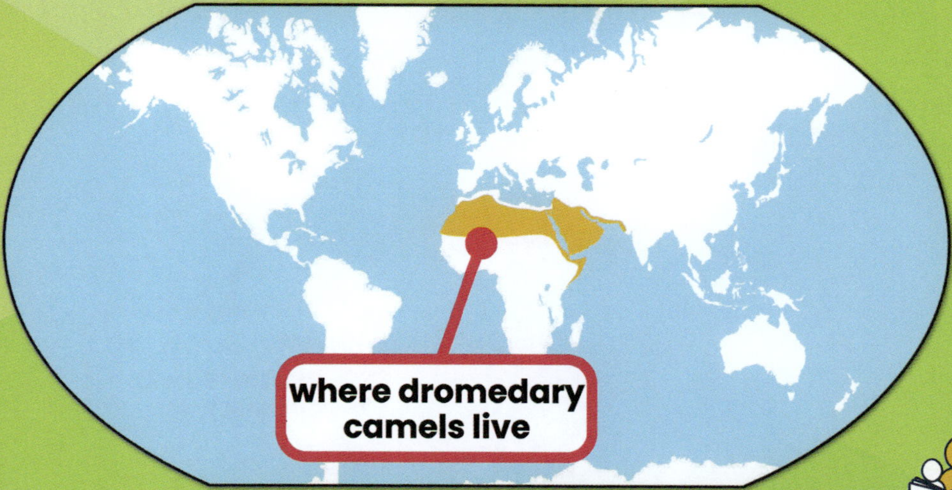

Some camels live in rocky deserts or on plains.

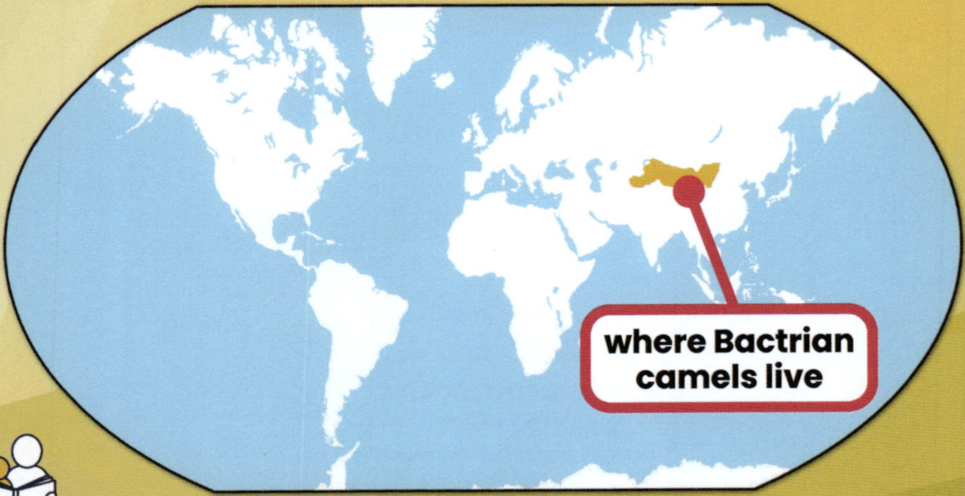

Bactrian camels live in Central and East Asia. They live in rocky deserts or on dry plains called **steppe**. The climate is very hot in the summer and very cold in the winter. In the winter, Bactrian camels grow thicker coats of fur to keep them warm. When temperatures rise again in the spring, they shed the extra hair.

Bactrian camels with their winter coats

Most camels live with people.

Nearly all camels today are **domesticated**, which means they are kept by humans. People have been herding camels for thousands of years. They ride camels or use their strong backs to carry heavy loads. People also use camels as a source of milk, meat, and hair. The only wild camels left are Bactrian camels that live in the Gobi Desert, which stretches across Mongolia and China.

What Camels Do

Camels eat plants.

Food is often scarce in the desert, so camels will eat almost any plants they can find. They eat grass, leaves, twigs, and stems. Their thick lips even let them eat thorny plants that most animals wouldn't be able to touch without hurting themselves.

Camels can go a long time without food or water.

Thanks to the fat stored in their humps, camels can survive months without food if they have to. They can also go more than a week without drinking, which comes in handy in the desert. They get some moisture from the plants they eat, and when they do drink water, they make it count. They can drink a lot of water at once and make it last them a long time. They also do not sweat, which keeps them from losing moisture in the desert heat.

Camels can travel far and fast.

Camels have been used for cross-desert travel for so long because they can walk up to 100 miles without needing to stop for food or water. They are also fast runners. They can reach speeds of 40 miles (64.3 km) per hour.

Camels live in groups.

A group of camels can be called a herd, a caravan, or a flock. The main herd is made up of the one adult male, the females, and the young camels. The other adult male camels form their own smaller group called a "bachelor herd."

Camels are very social animals. They communicate with many different sounds. They also like to say "hello" by blowing in each other's faces.

Camels have babies called calves.

When a mother camel is about to have a calf, she leaves the herd and finds a spot by herself. When a camel is born, it weighs 50-80 pounds (22.7-36.3 kg) and does not have a hump yet. A calf can begin to walk on its own about 30 minutes after it is born and can run within just a few hours. The mother camel and the calf rejoin the herd after about two weeks. Camels are fully grown when they are around seven years old.

Glossary

Bactrian camel

Camel with two humps; lives in Central and East Asia

Calf

Baby camel

Domesticated

Tamed to live with humans

Dromedary camel

Camel with one hump; lives in the Middle East

Steppe

Dry plains

Index

Credits

Check out these other titles in the Read Together series!

All About Camels

All About Cheetahs

All About Giraffes

All About Elephants

All About Kangaroos